MW01283423

THE BEGINNER'S GUIDE TO FPV

Alex Protogerellis

Alex Protogerellis
The beginner's guide to FPV
Second edition (b&w)

ISBN: 978-1-300-82000-0

© 2014, Alex Protogerellis
aproto.ecom@gmail.com

A big thank you to the FPV community across the globe – wouldn't have even discovered my passion without you!

Also, many thanks to Alex Greve (aka IBCrazy) for his insightful review of the first edition of this book.

Contents

1. About the author and about this book

This book is truly a beginner's guide to First Person View piloting. It intends to bring the reader from zero knowledge of the subject to a position where they can safely conduct FPV flights. It does not intend to give in-depth knowledge of every FPV topic but it will equip you with a good enough foundation to undertake your own research and make sense of what you read. It will also help you avoid some of the many pitfalls that come with the hobby.

I first started FPV a mere three and a half years ago and have spent many an evening and weekend researching, designing, building, flying and indeed crashing FPV. I started off with zero knowledge of the subject and I now fly safely at reasonably long range.

So clearly this guide has not been written by a pro (not that there are many pros in such a young hobby). It has been written by a hobbyist for hobbyists. All guidance within is based on personal experience and the very significant bulk of knowledge of other FPV pilots across the globe.

One unique aspect of the hobby is the pace at which it has developed over the last few years. When I first started researching there were a handful of vendors and a few hundred people who flew FPV across the globe. Now there are dozens of dedicated FPV vendors, aircraft specifically designed for FPV and even all-in-one FPV packages sold in toy shops. As a result, by the time you read this guide it is likely that while all concepts, principles and good practice will absolutely be valid, the detailed specifications and products will have advanced. So what you won't find in this guide is an equipment list and while I don't endorse any specific vendors I will reference and use photographs of specific products where appropriate.

Finally, while very much a beginner's guide to FPV, this is not a beginner's guide to radio controlled modelling, construction or flying. A reasonable level of prior knowledge is assumed. However, where FPV requirements necessitate changes to common practice these will be set out in detail.

2. The basics

2.1. What is FPV?

First person view piloting is the hobby of piloting a remote controlled vehicle beyond the line of sight[1] using an on-board camera. In its simplest form FPV is simply an on-board camera with a transmitter[2] and a ground station[3] monitor screen with a receiver[4].

While the majority of FPV pilots use planes, multicopters or helicopters there are many permutations such as cars and boats. As such, throughout this book reference will be made to "airplane", "flying" and "pilot", however these references can easily be replaced by "car", "driving" and "driver".

The hobby itself combines equal amounts of careful design, planning and construction of the FPV vehicle and piloting.

2.2. How difficult and how expensive is FPV?

FPV can be very tough and very expensive or just as easy and costly as standard RC modelling.

Complete ready to fly FPV packages can be bought for 350$ including airplane with camera and transmitter and control with video receiver and monitor.

However, a lot of the magic in FPV is building and improving your own FPV setup, incrementally making it more reliable, longer range, more versatile etc. This is something that does take knowledge, does occasionally end up in broken or lost planes and can end up costing from a few hundred to a few thousand dollars.

A basic (but very effective and very enjoyable) FPV setup can easily be built with 500$. More features (e.g. on screen display), better range (e.g. via antenna tracking), higher reliability (e.g. via long range control systems) will add to the cost.

---

[1] Flying close enough to be able to see the RC plane

[2] Transmitters are lightweight and currently analogue, capable of transmitting video and audio over the air. Typical frequencies are 900MHz, 1.3GHz, 2.4GHz and 5.8GHz. Refer to section 5.2 for more details.

[3] Ground station is the collection of equipment that stays close to the pilot and includes as a minimum the receiver and monitor or goggles. Refer to section 6 for more details.

[4] Receivers are devices that receive video and audio signals from the on-board transmitters and output a standard PAL or NTSC video signal and standard stereo audio. Refer to section 5.3 for more details

2.3. Safety and legality

Safety is paramount when flying any kind of radio controlled model and this is true of FPV. This means being conscious of your surroundings, never flying close to people or property and keeping out flight paths. If these guidelines and common sense are followed, FPV is a very safe hobby.

FPV is a new and rapidly developing hobby and as such legislation across the globe is very different and has various levels of maturity across different countries. In some countries specific legislation has been passed for FPV while in others FPV is covered by pre-existing legislation. What is legal in one country may not be legal in another. Typical restrictions apply to frequency used to transmit video (e.g. 900MHz is not legal in all countries), the altitude and distance from the pilot, the power level of the on-board transmitter, the location itself and other factors.

Always research the legal restrictions in your location before flying.

2.4. Sources of information

The very best source of information is the online communities of fellow FPV pilots. Online forums specifically include more or less the totality of publicly available FPV information and knowledge. It does take time to wade through the information but the breadth and depth is unparalleled. At the time of writing, of specific mention are www.fpvlab.com and www.rcgroups.com. There are of course a number of other FPV forums, a lot of them country specific.

Another great source of information are online shops and vendor websites. Browsing the available products gives you a great idea of the kit available. Including a list of vendors in this guide, whilst tempting, would only result it the list being out of date in no time. Instead, one of the most comprehensive list of FPV vendors can be found at the sponsor's gate at fpvlab.com.

2.5. What is FPV – in more detail

As mentioned in section 2.1, First Person View (or First Person Video) is the hobby of piloting a standard radio controlled plane through an on-board camera, providing a pilot's view of the world. It enables the pilot to experience the thrill of virtually being on board the plane and fly beyond the normal line of site.

In its simplest form FPV can be comprised of the following components:
  a. The plane itself: Any radio controlled plane (or other vehicle) counts. This should come with a method of controlling (whether a standard RC controller or otherwise)
  b. A small camera: This is the type typically used for security systems. They are small, robust and light
  c. A video transmitter and its antenna: The transmitter will take the video feed form the camera and beam it down to the pilot on the ground

d. A video receiver and its antenna: The receiver will receive the video feed from the video transmitter and make it available to the pilot's viewing device

e. A viewing device: This can be a small LCD monitor like the ones used for in-car DVD players, video goggles typically used for computer gaming or even a full plasma television

This simple setup enables the hobbyist to virtually sit in the pilot's cockpit and experience the FPV sensation.

More complex systems can give the pilot greater range, more information or more reliability but are not necessary for FPV piloting.

2.6. Tools

For the average FPV pilot the hobby doesn't need any special tools (other than tools used for standard RC modelling). However, given the amount of custom work pilots typically do to their planes it is useful to have some of the following at your disposal:

a. An affordable multimeter: A common issue with a new setup is "it just doesn't work". Diagnosing the problem is much easier with a multimeter. You'll be able to see which cables are live, what voltage is produced by which devices as well as get an indication of the signal of video and servo wires

b. Cable stripper and servo plug crimper: It is common for pilots to create their own cables in order to make them exactly the right length for their setup. Putting plugs on wires without a proper crimper is frustrating and usually unreliable. Saving 20$ on a crimper may cost you a few hundred in an out of control plane

c. Velcro, double sided tape and hot glue are all good ways of attaching components to the fuselage, giving both secure fastening and a degree of flexibility

d. A small powertool (such as a Dremel) will make life much easier when drilling or cutting aircraft or components

e. Radio frequency meter or electrosmog meter. These devices can give you detailed information on the signals passing through the airwaves or just an overall level of electronic radiation. This can be useful for understanding whether your gear is transmitting but also for scoping whether a potential flight sight has a lot of interference. Really basic meters cost around $50 but don't provide much insight. More useful and frequency specific ones can cost a few hundred.

2.7. Some numbers

Some of the first questions prospective pilots ask is "how far", "how high", "how powerful", "how long" and so on. The answer to all these questions is "it depends on the equipment, flight area and many other parameters". However, to provide some perspective, the following table attempts to set out some high level answers to these questions. Do not use any of this as a rule as the answer truly is "it depends"!

Question	Depends on	Low	Medium	High	Insane
How far can my plane go?	Control and video link and battery duration	0.5km - 2km is a common range with basic gear	2km – 5km is a common range with a good setup, in good conditions and some advanced equipment	5km – 10km is easily achievable with enough experience and long range gear	50km plus has been achieved by some of the masters of the hobby
How high can my plane go?	A plane can fly as high as legal limitations and control and video range will allow (see previous row)				
How powerful is the video/control signal?	Legal limitations, transmitter power	10mw	500mw	1000mw	Over 1000mw
How long can the plane fly for?	Battery capacity, plane type	5 minutes	15 minutes	30 minutes	Tens of hours

2.8. Basic components

It takes a number of components for an operational FPV setup. This section sets out, at a high level, the basic components that are required. While described separately, often these components are interlinked. For example an on-screen display module[5] may also take over control of the aircraft under certain circumstances.

The basic components of any FPV vehicle are as follows:

2.8.1. The vehicle itself

Quite an obvious component but one that takes a lot of decisions, design and preparation. Any vehicle could be made into an FPV vehicle but in doing so there are certain considerations:

a. Positioning: Positioning of the components on the vehicle is critical as interference between them can be disastrous

b. Reliability: While for every RC vehicle reliability is desirable, this is much more significant in the case of FPV where a crash could happen far away from the pilot and involve some expensive equipment

c. Field of view: The most common type of RC plane (propeller in the front) is the least common in FPV as the propeller can partly block the camera view. As such twin-motor or rear motor (pusher) planes are often used

d. Carrying capacity: FPV equipment tends to add considerable weight to an aircraft, especially if long flight times and large batteries are desired. As such the weight carrying capacity of the plane is important

2.8.2. The video link

This enables the video from on-board the vehicle to be transmitted and then viewed by the pilot on the ground in practically real time. The video link, as a minimum, is composed of:

a. The on-board camera: This is a light weight camera that can be powered by DC current and which outputs a video signal. Currently these are CMOS or CCD, mainly colour cameras that work on 5 or 12 volt and which output standard definition analogue (PAL/NTSC) video. In the future it is likely that digital high definition signal may be possible

b. The on-board video transmitter (VTx): This component is powered by DC current and receives the video and audio signal and broadcasts it at a specific frequency

c. The on-board video transmitter antenna: This is classed as a separate component. There are many choices of antennas (and a whole science/art), each providing different characteristics of performance under different circumstances (e.g. some antennas are great if the plane is flying straight but very poor if the plane banks or turns frequently)

---

[5] An additional piece of on-board equipment which overlays live flight data (such as airspeed) on your video

d. The ground station receiver antenna: Just like the on-board video transmitter antenna, the receiver antenna is hugely important

e. The ground station receiver (VRx): This component is powered by DC current, receives video and audio signals from the airplane via the antenna and outputs video and audio signal. Currently this is analogue (PAL/NTSC) and standard definition

f. The ground station monitor or goggles: This is the last component of the video link and transfers the video signal to the pilot's eyes. LCD or similar screens are typically used while goggles offer a more immersive perspective

2.8.3. The radio control link

This is the link that enables the pilot to control the aircraft. At its simplest it is just a standard radio control link (e.g. an old school 72MHz radio). More complex setups include special transmitter modules and receivers to enable much longer range and more reliable flights.

2.8.4. Enhancements

There is an endless array of enhancements that can be applied to a standard FPV setup to make it more reliable, capable or enjoyable. These are described in later sections but here is a sampling:

a. On-board high definition camera: This enables recording of flight video at high definition, making it ideal for viewing later

b. Ground station recorder: A device that records the live video feed from the airplane

c. On screen display: A component that uses sensors (e.g. GPS) and displays additional data as an overlay over the live video feed. This can include altitude and speed, battery capacity, coordinates and which way is "home"

d. Head tracking: A setup that enables the pilot to control where the on-board camera is facing by moving his head – giving the ultimate immersive experience

e. Antenna tracking: An useful component for longer range flights, the tracker ensures that the ground station antenna is always pointing towards the airplane

f. Lost plane beacon: If worse comes to worse this device can help you locate your lost plane using standard walkie talkies or a mobile phone and google maps

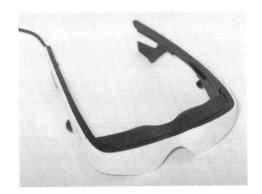
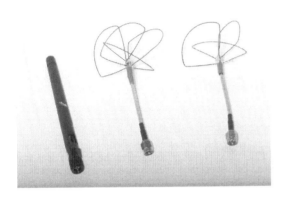
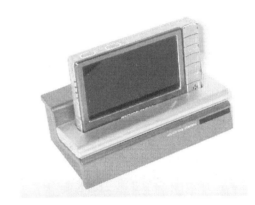

Figure 1: A collection of FPV gear

2.8.5. An example setup

The following diagram represents a relatively advanced setup utilising a lot of the components that are discussed throughout this guide. Don't worry if some of them appear complicated or confusing – that's what the rest of the guide is here for!

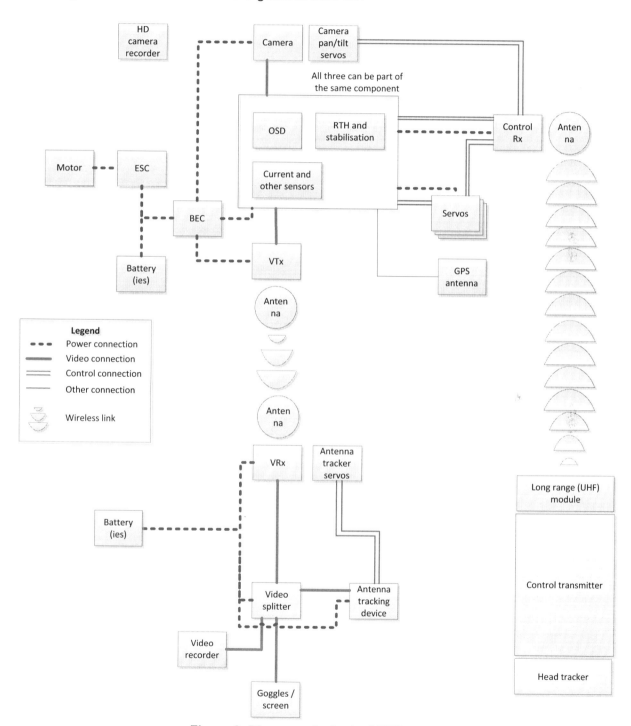

Figure 2: Diagram of a typical FPV setup

2.9. Your first setup... and building up

As with many things, the old adage "Keep it simple stupid" holds true. Typically, the more components you add to your system the more complex it becomes and the more chance for incompatibilities or mistakes to happen. And don't forget, usually an FPV setup has multiple single points of failure (or, to be more exact, almost every component represents a single point of failure), so, the fewer the components, the lower the chance of failure.

Having said this however, there are some components which, while optional, do greatly reduce the chance of things going wrong or, if they do go wrong, greatly improve the chances of recovery.

There are many schools of thought about what the best first setup is and how to progress from then on. Below I'll setup an approach which I feel works well.

Step 1 – Research
This is the most important step and, as you're reading this guide, you've already started. Research your setup until you're 100% confident you understand how it works. If you leave anything to luck it's likely that it will eventually go wrong.

Step 2 – Build a decent RC plane
This step could be combined with the next step but unless you're very confident of you standard-RC plane building skills it is recommended that you do them separately. In this step you need to build your non-FPV RC plane and ensure that it works reliably. However, do build it with your FPV equipment in mind as some modifications to the plane may be required at this stage to fit the necessary gear.

It is much cheaper and less time consuming to realise that CG[6] mistake or that cracked motor mount before you've installed your FPV gear.

Step 3 – Your first FPV build
Now the exciting stuff begins... While the first setup could be as simple as a camera, transmitter, receiver and monitor, two additional components are recommended to make the flight safer.

Specifically, it is advisable to install an on-screen display (OSD) module on the plane that will display navigation data on your video stream and can help you navigate home (the first few flights can be disorienting). An OSD, when equipped with a GPS, can display the plane's coordinates, helping the pilot recover the plane if worse comes to worse.

Additionally, a ground station recorder is a highly advisable early addition, enabling the pilot to record the flights (this could be a dedicated digital video recorder, a laptop with video capture capability or an old camcorder).

---

[6] Centre of gravity

The full equipment list looks something like this:

a. The plane you've built and tested in step 2, including its RC control link equipment (RC transmitter and receiver)
b. On-board camera
c. On-board on screen display (with GPS sensor)
d. On-board transmitter with rubber duck[7] antenna
e. (if required, depending on the voltage differential between the flight battery[8] and the FPV equipment requirements) Secondary on-board battery (specifically for FPV gear) or voltage regulator (or BEC) for stepping down the main battery voltage to the voltage required for the FPV equipment
f. Ground station receiver with rubber duck antenna[9]
g. Ground station video splitter to split the single incoming video signal into two
h. Ground station video recorder (e.g. laptop)
i. Monitor or goggles

This setup will enable you to fly with confidence, at relatively low cost and will be a great platform for expanding your setup in the future.

Two fundamental principles:
a. Fit your setup to your wallet: It is very tempting to buy more kit and get more functionality by buying cheaper components. Time and time again it has been proven that this leads to lost or damaged planes and eventually buying high quality gear

b. Think ahead: Some components only work with each other if they are made by the same manufacturer (for example, in some cases, the OSD and antenna tracking components). So think and plan out your ideal setup from the outset to ensure you're building towards it

Step 4 – Your first "FPV" flight

Your first flight with your FPV equipment should not be done in first person view.

After thoroughly range checking your gear on the ground, undertake your first flight in non-FPV third person view. In doing so however have your FPV equipment operational and record the video on your ground station for close examination later.

This will enable you to determine whether your FPV gear has affected your control of the plane (which may be as simple as a change in CG or equipment interference) and whether your video signal is strong and clear.

---

[7] "Rubber duck" is the type of antenna most commonly included with video transmitter and receivers. You may want to immediately skip to a circularly polarised antenna such as the cloverleaf to greatly increase reliability with minimal extra cost or effort. See section 5.4 for more details

[8] The battery used to power the motor of the plane

[9] Note that if you've used a circular polarised cloverleaf for your VTx you'll need a similarly circular polarised antenna on your VRx. See section 5.4 for more details

Step 5 – Your first real FPV flight

Finally, the moment you've been waiting for – your first flight using all your FPV gear.

Although it will be very tempting to wonder far away, this first flight must be done while in line of site and with a "spotter"[10]. The first few flights can be quite disorienting (some people even get a feeling of vertigo) so here are a few steps you can take to make the experience less stressful:

a. Become familiar with the surrounding area. This will allow you to know where you are and where you need to be heading. Especially useful is google maps (satellite view) which lets you see the area from an FPV-like perspective

b. Launch the plane in 3rd person and, once comfortable, switch to FPV. Similarly, landing in 3rd person may be easier to begin with

c. Train your spotter. Confusions about what "left" and "right" mean can lead to additional stress. Let your spotter know what you want them to do and how you'd like them to guide you

d. Don't clutter your on screen display. Too much information can be confusing, reduce the usable image space and simply make the experience less enjoyable

e. Familiarise yourself with the on screen information and make sure you know where the key items such are the "home arrow" and altimeter are

Step 6 – Flights 2 to 6 (or so)

The next few flights should be all about becoming accustomed to FPV flying. By the end of it you should know your equipment and its behaviour inside out and not stress (as much) during flying. By this point you will have reached the limited range of your equipment and will want a bit more freedom

Step 7 – Longer range

By this point you should have your own view about what your next step should be. My suggestion would be to increase your range to enable more comfortable, longer and more interesting flights.

When doing so remember that flight range depends on the range of the video link and, much more importantly, the control link. Your effective range is the lesser of the two.

I suggest three incremental additions at this stage:

a. Replace your "rubber duck" antennas with cloverleaf, skew planar or other non-directional circular polarised antennas. This is cheap, simple and greatly increases the range of your video. See section 5.4 for more details

b. Change your control link to UHF (subject to legal restrictions). This will guarantee a reliable control signal way beyond your video link. See section 4.3 for more information

c. Replace your receiver antenna with a higher gain, directional circular polarised antenna on an antenna tracker. This will vastly increase your video range

---

[10] A spotter is a friend who is not using FPV gear and who can see the plane in 3rd person view, guiding the pilot as required

With these improvements you should have a minimum range from a few kilometres to over 10 kilometers – which is more than enough for most pilots for a long time (actually, a lot of very experienced pilots prefer flying at closer range and closer to the ground – its much more exciting!)

Step 8 – The final and endless step

By this point you should be a seasoned FPV pilot. How you expand your setup will be up to you and could include return to home (autopilot), stabilisation, head tracking, night flying, a more agile or bigger airplane and more.

3. The FPV vehicle

This section sets out the types of FPV vehicles that are commonly used and the main characteristics of each. It also provides guidance on the correct positioning of components on the vehicle, cabling, considerations for choosing some of the standard RC components, information on batteries and voltage and finally a description of some additional "gadgets" you can consider for your setup.

3.1. The vehicle

The FPV vehicle can be anything as long as it can carry the equipment and can be controlled remotely. Your dog could be an FPV vehicle with a camera on its head and some complex bone on a stick on a servo kind of setup!

Lately even size has not been a limitation, with nano FPV multicopters and airplanes being achievable using tiny batteries, cameras and transmitters. Note that all principles and guidelines that apply to normal-sized craft also apply to nano scale ones.

3.1.1. Airplanes

Airplanes are the most popular FPV vehicle due to their carrying capacity, speed and great views from above. There is a plethora of appropriate choices of airplane although a few models are currently more popular than others (the more popular choices are referenced below but by no means do they represent the only, or the best, options).

In choosing an airplane you will need to consider:

Figure 3: A classic twin motor plane

a. Size: The larger the airplane the better it will handle in winds (usually) and the more weight it will be able to carry. However, a large plane necessitates a larger aircraft carrier (i.e. car) and launch site. Typical wingspan is one to two meters.

b. Construction: The three main choices are traditional balsa, foam and plastic/fibreglass. Foam is the most popular due to its durability and customisability and comes in many different types (EPO, EPP, etc), each with its own characteristics. Fibre or plastic planes can give a smoother flight but can be heavier and more prone to damage. Balsa planes are not commonly chosen due to the results of even slightly rough landings

c. Type: There are a number of very different choices here which we'll expand on below

The standard airplane

This is the common type of airplane with motor in the middle front. There is a huge choice of these in all sizes and attitudes, from trainers to 3D aerobatic planes. The main issue however is the fact that the propeller is most likely to be in view of the camera, limiting the usable view.

A solution to this is planes with two (or more) motors on the wings such as the popular Multiplex Twinstar II.

Pusher planes

These are standard planes with the motor and propeller behind the CG, effectively pushing (as opposed to pulling) the plane. These are very common (a classic example is the Easystar) and while pusher planes are just slightly less efficient than pullers, the compromise is worth it.

When choosing a pusher plane watch out for the limited propeller size. If you're after a long range aircraft then you'll want a large two blade propeller with a small pitch and in pusher planes the body of the plane will limit the prop size.

Figure 4: A classic "pusher" plane

Jets

FPV jets are flown but are not for the feint hearted. They are certainly not suggested for the beginner pilot (whether beginner to RC or to FPV).

Flying wings

Flying wings have recently become very popular in the FPV community. They offer a good balance of desirable characteristics including:

    a. Very durable (they're just a big slab of foam)
    b. Very reliable (minimum moving parts)
    c. Good carrying capacity
    d. Fast and agile, making for exciting FPV

They are not for everyone however. If you want slower laid back flights, have limited storage or transport space or are really keen to have a rudder (most wings don't have rudder control) then a pusher may be more appropriate.

Figure 5: A classic flying wing

3.1.2. Multicopters

A recent introduction to the RC world, multicopters are increasingly the FPV vehicle of choice for many pilots. They offer precision flying, good carrying capacity and can be flown within a limited area. They are also commonly used for professional videography with the use of camera stabilising gimbals.

While they offer great versatility and a unique flying experience, multicopters do tend to be more expensive than planes and involve more complex electronics in tighter space. They also tend to crash much harder as they don't glide – so a handsome repair budget is advisable.

There are many choices of multicopter and the main decisions will be around the size (hence carrying capacity) and number of motors.

Please refer to section 11.3 (Special considerations for multicopters).

Figure 6: A nano FPV quad copter

Figure 7: A full sized quad copter

3.1.3. Helicopters

Helicopters offer a similar experience to multicopters but tend to be more mechanically sophisticated, capable of more complex manoeuvres and tend to require more advanced piloting skills.

3.1.4. Car/boat

Cars and boats of all kinds are also occasionally used for FPV, offering a very different experience to aerial platforms. With ground and water vehicles weight is less of an issue and the primary concern is choice of appropriate video link to cater for the environment in which the car/boat is driven. Line of sight between the ground station and the vehicle will usually be obstructed and as such issues such as multipath[11] will be even more important than usual. As such it is advisable to use circular polarised antennas and avoid 5.8GHz link which doesn't perform well with obstacles.

3.2. Advice on non-FPV stuff

When building your plane all good practice guidelines for a reliable build apply. As FPV planes go beyond the line of site and tend to cost a lot more than traditional RC planes it is advisable to only choose the most reliable components. Specifically it is advisable to:

a. Use an independent BEC for providing 5 or 6 volt power to your servos and other components. While most ESCs have a built-in BEC the power demands of FPV gear tend to necessitate a separate BEC. This also gives the added benefit of maintaining control of the aircraft even if the ESC has malfunctioned or over heated.
b. Use high quality metal gear servos. The additional cost may save your plane
c. Use a high quality ESC and motor which are more than capable of handling the load that you expect them to have to bear

3.3. All important positioning

Positioning of components on an FPV craft can make or break an FPV setup. Poor positioning can lead to unreliable control or video link and potentially disaster. This happens because some of the components may interfere with others.

A lot of this pain can be avoided if three guidelines are followed:

---

[11] A specific kind of signal interference. Refer to section 7 for more details.

a. The VTx should be placed as far as possible from all other equipment. VTx are high power devices that produce strong signals. Keep them away from sensitive devices such as your control receiver and GPS receiver

b. All receivers should be kept away from sources of electromagnetic radiation of any kind. This applies to the control receiver and the GPS receiver. These should be placed as far away from the VTx as possible but also away from the ESC and motor

c. If you do detect the symptoms of interference (glitchy control or bad quality video at short range) do a meticulous trial and error analysis to locate the culprit component. The culprit could even be entirely innocent looking components such as a small voltage regulator, your GoPro[12] or a servo

---

[12] GoPro Hero is the most popular make of on-board high definition recording camera

3.4.   Batteries and voltage (filters etc)

Most FPV setups will require power in at least two voltage levels, the voltage required for the motor (lets say 12V) and the voltage required for the FPV gear (lets say 5V). As such your setup should be able to cater for both. This can be done in two ways, either by providing two separate batteries (each of the correct voltage required) or by using some kind of voltage regulator to increase or decrease voltage.

Be very careful when choosing a voltage regulator as some are known to cause significant interference (one of my early crashes was due to a voltage step-down freezing the 72MHz control link unexpectedly). Read reviews in the FPV forums to ensure compatibility. A common way of stepping down is the use of a BEC.

Whether or not to use two separate sets of batteries, one for flight and one for control and FPV equipment is a matter of debate as both approaches have their merits. The main pros and cons of a dual battery setup[13] are listed below:

Pros	Cons
a. If the flight battery is exhausted (which can happen as the flight battery is the one that determines flight time) you will retain control of the plane and may be able to safely glide it home b. If the flight battery is exhausted and the plane crashes then you may still be able to use the video signal (assuming you have an OSD with GPS coordinates) to locate your vehicle c. It avoids a lot of "dirty" power issues by isolating the ESC circuit (see below)	a. Introduces an additional single point of failure. If either battery has an issue then the whole plane is at risk b. Most setups only monitor the voltage of the motor battery because, in theory, the second battery will far outlast the motor one. But if it doesn't all systems will fail with no warning c. One more battery to charge

Another consideration when powering your setup is video distortion caused by "dirty" power. A power system that powers an ESC (for example), if also used to power video systems may result in distortion to the video. An LC filter[14] can be used in these cases to "clean" the power feeding the video gear.

Figure 8: An LC filter

---

[13] One for power to the ESC/motor and one for control and FPV equipment
[14] A small device that can be interjected in the middle of a power cable to "clean" the power

3.5. Cabling

An FPV setup has a lot of cables: Video cables, servo cables, sensor cables and power cables. As such it is common for pilots to create their own cables so that they are perfectly matched to their setup and vehicle. When doing so basic guidance is as follows:

a. The shorter the cables the better. As such try to take the shortest route between components
b. Twisted cables are better. Twisted cables (e.g. a servo cable who's three individual cables (signal, power and ground) are twisted) offer better resistance to interference
c. For a very robust setup some pilots use shielded cables which absorb incoming and outgoing electrons. This however is certainly not a necessity for most setups
d. Ferrite rings can be used to remove some interference. Only use them where required as they add some extra weight

When cabling you FPV plane care must be taken to avoid ground loops. As this is an advanced topic it can be found in section 11.2 (Ground loops)

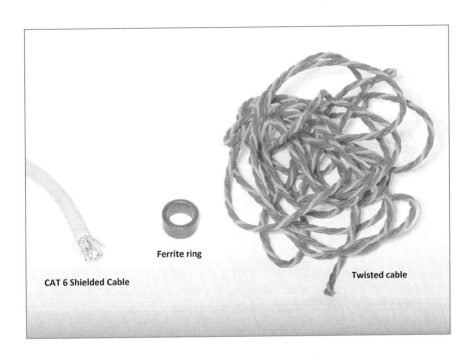

Ferrite ring

CAT 6 Shielded Cable

Twisted cable

Figure 9: Various methods of protecting from interference

3.6. Other gadgets

This section covers some of the common "gadgets" that can be useful in an FPV setup

3.6.1. Independent beacon

It is always good to have multiple methods of tracking your vehicle if lost. An independent tracker can be one of those methods. These are devices that are powered separately from all other components and allow you to locate your vehicle hours or days after it has been lost.

Two common forms are the UHF tracker and the GPS/GSM tracker. See section 9 for more details.

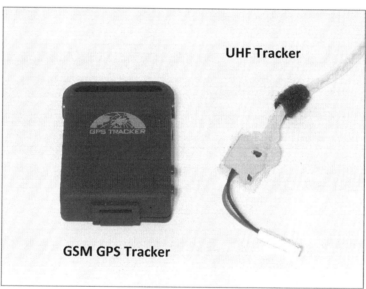

Figure 10: Two types of locating beacon

3.6.2. Lighting

LED lighting can be added to a plane either to make it more visible (for safety reasons or for night flying) or to light up the ground when flying at night.

Complex water cooled LED setups have been created that produce a significant amount of light, enabling the pilot to confidently pilot at night.

4. Controlling your plane

There are a number of frequencies and technologies that can be used for the control link. The choice of link depends on the desired range as well as legal limitations. Irrespective of these the golden rule is to never have the same (or similar) frequency for both video link and control link. As such pilots who use 2.4GHz for control will not use 2.4GHz for the video link.

4.1. "Old school" 35 or 72MHz

35MHz and 72MHz are the frequencies used for RC control for the last few decades. They necessitate a long antenna both on the transmitter and receiver and tend to provide a reliable link for 1-2km. 35/72MHz is generally more reliable than 2.4GHz for short and medium range but less appropriate than UHF for long range.

4.2. 2.4GHz

2.4GHz is the current standard in RC control with all major makes producing their main range of transmitters and receivers at 2.4GHz. However, for FPV purposes and depending on the make in question, 2.4GHz can be unreliable at anything but the shortest ranges (i.e. within line of sight). This is due to the high level of competition in the frequency (primarily from computer WiFi), high susceptibility of some receivers to interference and the nature of digital control which can lock-out the pilot (as opposed to experiencing glitches with analogue control).

Because of all this it is generally not advised to control FPV craft with 2.4GHz for medium or long distance. It could suit for the very first couple of flights within line of sight but should quickly be replaced with a more reliable solution (72MHz or UHF). Also note that while boosters do exist to boost the power of 2.4GHz systems, the same concerns still apply.

4.3. UHF (433MHz)

UHF systems are the most reliable systems for long range. A number of options exist (such as DragonLink, EasyUHF and TSLRS), all of which offer a spread spectrum, reliable connection for over 10km.

UHF systems typically utilise standard 2.4GHz radios (e.g. a standard Futaba) but replace their standard transmitter module with a UHF module. This is achieved either by utilising the trainer port of the transmitter to transfer the signal to the UHF device or by removing the 2.4GHz module and plugging or soldering the UHF one.

Be aware that a common limitation when using the trainer port (which uses PPM signal) is a restriction of the number of channels, commonly to a maximum of 8. UHF systems also come with a specialised on-board UHF receiver, typically capable of 12 channels. Be aware that some components (e.g. certain cameras) can cause interference on the UHF band. So research your camera to ensure it will not limit your control range.

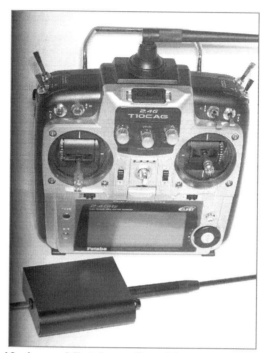

Figure 11: A 10 channel Futaba radio with a UHF long range module

4.4. How many channels do I need

Standard RC piloting typically requires no more than 4 radio channels. However, in FPV you will soon find that even 8 channels may not be enough. A typical setup may require some or all of the below:

a. Throttle, ailerons, elevator, rudder
b. Flaps
c. Camera switch (to switch between two cameras)
d. Lighting control
e. Pan servo for panning the camera
f.   Tilt servo for tilting the camera
g. 2 x channels (or more) for interfacing with the OSD

4.5. Return to home and stabilisation

Return to home systems enable the plane to auto pilot itself back to the place where it was launched. This may happen on the pilot's command or if the radio link is lost. This is an important safety feature to ensure that even if the control or video link is lost (due to range, battery, ground station or other malfunction) the plane will return to the point of launch and circle over head (or even land itself), enabling the pilot to land it in 3rd person view.

Return to home systems are typically integrated with OSD systems and use the same sensors (GPS, altimeter, airspeed sensor etc.) to understand the location and behaviour of the plane. Typically the receiver's control outputs (e.g. elevator, throttle and aileron) will be connected to the RTH system and that in turn to the relevant servos. In normal flight the receiver's commands will be transferred unaltered to the servos but in RTH mode, the receiver signals will be ignored and the RTH system will drive the throttle and servos.

For many RTH systems to be effective, it is also necessary to employ a stabilisation system (either integrated with the RTH or independent). Stabilisation systems utilise accelerometers and gyros to determine the pitch and yaw of a plane and then alter the servo signals to return the plane to a completely horizontal position. This enables the RTH system to control the direction and speed of flight and the stabilisation system to ensure the plane is flying level and straight.

Stabilisation systems can also be used to support flight when in control of the pilot. This can be configured in many ways but commonly the stabilisation system will return the plane to level flight whenever the elevator and aileron sticks are centred.

Note that RTH systems typically require a lot of configuration and trial and error before they can be trusted to bring the plane back safely.

4.6. RSSI

Remote signal strength indicator (RSSI) is a signal output by some receivers that indicates how strong the control link is. This is typically a voltage level between two levels (which indicate no signal and perfect signal). The RSSI output by the control receiver can be processed and displayed by some OSDs to inform the pilot when their control signal is getting weak.

4.7. Antennas

Much like the video link, a selection of antennas are available for the control link with choices at the Tx including standard monopoles, the moxon and yagi and choices at the receiver end including monopole, dipole and turnstile. Please refer to the antennas section for more details.

5. The video link

The video link is essentially what differentiates a standard radio controlled plane from an FPV plane as it delivers the on-board (first person) view from the plane to the pilot.

Key components of the video link are the on-board camera, the video transmitter and its antenna, the video receiver and its antenna and the monitor or goggles used to view the signal (which is covered in the next chapter).

The video is transmitted between the plane and the pilot using radio waves (such as the ones used by mobile phones or computer wireless networks). The quality and robustness of this transmission is possibly the most important aspect of FPV (alongside the control link).

A wide array of factors can affect the quality of the video link, including:
a. The distance between the video transmitter (VTx) and the video receiver (VRx)
b. The frequency used (e.g. 2.4GHz)
c. The antennas used on the transmitter and receiver and their orientation
d. Interference on the plane or on the ground (i.e. ambient interference)
e. The power of the VTx
f. Obstacles and objects between and around the VTx and VRx (see Frensel zone below)

While understanding RF theory is not a necessity for being successful at FPV, some understanding of basic concepts and how they should be applied in practice is invaluable. This section provides a good grounding in these concepts while section 11.1 (Link margin) provides a more advanced loop at the topic..

One such concept is the Frensel zone. In simple terms, the Frensel zone is an area the shape of a rugby ball between the transmitter and the receiver. To achieve the best link this area should be free of obstacles. As obstacles are introduced, the link strength decreases with obstacles in the direct path between the VTx and VRx causing the largest interference.

The following diagram illustrates this point.

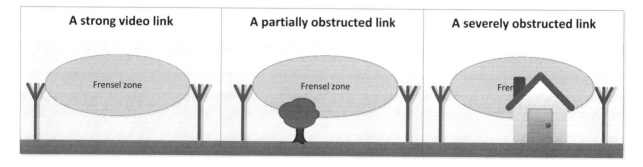

Further concepts such as polarisation and multipath are explained later in this section.

5.1. Frequencies

There are a number of frequencies and technologies that can be used for the video link. The choice of link depends on the desired range as well as legal limitations. Irrespective of these the golden rule is to never have the same (or similar) frequency for both video link and control link. As such pilots who use 2.4GHz for control will not use 2.4GHz for the video link.

A number of frequencies are used for the video link, each one having its own limitations and constraints. Typical frequencies and their characteristics are as follows:

a. 900MHz: In theory gives the longest range and necessitates larger antennas. However, it is often illegal and unreliable as this frequency is also used for mobile phones in most places

b. 1.2GHz (or 1.3GHz): A common choice for video link with very good range although options for kit may be more limited than 2.4GHz. Note that 1.2GHz equipment can interfere with UHF control systems, hence necessitate filtering (which is generally inexpensive)

c. 2.4GHz: Another common choice for video link, with many options for equipment. Note that this tends to be the noisiest band (due to computer WiFi) and also cannot be used if standard 2.4GHz control link is also used. Recently 2.3GHz has also emerged which is a less congested frequency.

d. 5.8GHz: This frequency is provides less range per miilliwatt of transmitter power. This is due to the signal being easily disrupted by objects and even moisture in the air. This is typically chosen due to legal limitations on other frequencies, the small size of antennas and being the least congested frequency. It is useful for short range flying (e.g. with nano planes or multicopters).

Note that within each frequency band there are a number of channels and as such your VTx and VRx should have not only the same frequency but also the same channel. Practically all VTx and VRx enable the selection of channel by using a switch or button.

5.2. Cameras

It is very common for FPV craft to carry two cameras: the flight camera by which the pilot can pilot the plane and a high definition video recorder to record the flight on on-board memory for viewing later. This section covers the standard considerations while section 11.4 (Alternative video links) provides details of some of the more exotic options.

5.2.1. The flight cam

Flight cams are typically small (smaller than a matchbox), low resolution cameras that output analogue video (PAL/NTSC). These typically use CCD or CMOS sensors and come in a variety of prices.

The two most important characteristics when choosing a flight cam are:

a. Resolution: This is typically measured in TV Lines and the higher the better. Note however that the resolution that the pilot will see also depends on the display resolution of the monitor or goggles that are used to view.
b. Handling of difficult light conditions: A flight cam must enable the pilot to see under a variety of conditions. A good flight cam will not black out the image when the sun is in view and will not darken the image beyond use when a bright sky is in view

Additionally considerations and options include:

a. Voltage: Flight cams are typically either 5V or 12V. Bear this in mind as you may need to step-up or step-down the voltage of your battery
b. Cased or not cased: Typically the same flight cam can be bought with a plastic case or without
c. Viewing angle: Flight cams can typically use a variety of lenses. Slightly wide angle lenses tend to be preferable as they offer a wider field of view
d. Night flying: Specific cameras (often monochrome) are specially designed for night flying, providing much higher sensitivity than normal cameras

Figure 12: A standard flight camera

5.2.2. The HD cam

The flight cam, while perfect for piloting, does not provide high resolution. As such FPV setups typically include a high definition video camera which records HD video onto an on-board memory card which is then retrieved when the plane has landed. While normal camcorders can be used, extreme sports cams such as the GoPro Hero are preferred due to their small size.

Some HD cams also provide a video out feature which outputs analogue video out. This enables

Figure 13: A GoPro Hero, one of the more popular HD recorders

30

these cameras to be used for both HD recording and as the flight cam. If you choose to do this make sure that the specific HD cam is fit for piloting. While there are two schools of thought on this matter, common concerns include:

a. Lag: The analogue output of some HD cams can introduce a small lag (delay) which, depending on the type of flying, can be an issue
b. Handling of light conditions and overall quality: Many HD cams do not handle difficult lighting conditions as well as dedicated flight cams and also may produce inferior quality analogue video
c. Reliability: HD cameras are complex devices which may introduce additional failure points (e.g. if the battery runs out, if the camera switches modes mid-flight etc)

5.2.3. Other options

Pan and tilt

A common addition to many setups is the ability to control where the camera is pointing using two servos (one for pan and one for tilt). This makes the experience more immersive and interesting. Pan/tilt can be applied to just the flight cam or to both the flight and HD cams together.

This is controlled via two receiver channels and either through sliders or dials on the transmitter or via the use of headtracking (see below).

Figure 14: A pan/tilt pod for both HD recorder and flight cam

Head tracking

Head trackers are devices that enable the pilot to control the pan/tilt of the camera by moving their head. This makes for a very immersive experience where the pilot's head movements translate directly to movements of the on-board camera.

Head tracking is typically achieved with dedicated head tracking devices which are placed on the pilot's head (e.g. on the goggles or a cap). These use a combination of accelerometers, gyros and compasses to determine head movements.

The signals are then transferred to the transmitter via the trainer port, through soldering at appropriate points or, in the case of some UHF control transmitters, through a special headtracking port on the UHF device.

It is highly advisable not to attempt head tracking before you are very confident with all other aspects of FPV flying as it adds additional complexity, additional points of failure and can be disorienting at first.

Camera switch

When multiple flight cams are installed on the plane, camera switches enable the pilot to select which camera video will be transmitted to the ground. This is controlled through an additional receiver channel.

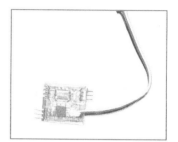

Figure 15: A simple camera switch

5.3. The VTx

The video transmitter receives the video signal from the camera (and audio signal from a microphone if available) and transmits it via radio waves to the ground. The main characteristics of a VTx are its frequency, power and input voltage.

VTx exist for transmitting at any of the possible FPV video link frequencies (see advice in section 5 for details on the various frequencies used).

They also come in a variety of power levels, from 10mW to over 1W. When choosing the power level of your transmitter you should take a number of factors into account:

a. Size: Although VTxs are generally lightweight, setting up micro or nano vehicles for FPV generally makes high power prohibitive
b. Range: While it is true that more power means more range, the two are not proportional. To double your range you need to quadruple the power, so after a certain point there are much better ways to increase video link range (e.g. by the use of directional receiver antennas)
c. Interference: As mentioned already, it is important to keep the VTx away from most other equipment due to the interference it can cause. Increasing the power will exacerbate this
d. Legal restrictions: Always ensure that your power level is within legal limits for the frequency and altitude of transmission

Figure 16: A 2.4GHz 500mW VTx (with added cooling)

Due to the above the most common power level is 500-600mW.

When installing the VTx, in addition to following the positioning advice in section 2.6 bear in mind that VTxs get quite hot and in many cases (especially if 500mW or more) should not be run on the ground without additional cooling for more than a few minutes. As such the side of the VTx with the cooling plate or heat sink should be exposed to airflow on your vehicle.

Finally, although VTx power does affect the achievable range, the most important determinant is the VTx and VRx antennas used (see below).

5.4. The VRx & diversity

Once the signal is transmitted by the VTx it is received by the video receiver of the same frequency. The VRx then outputs the video (and audio where available) via standard analogue PAL or NTSC signal and standard RCA cable (or 4-pole jack).

While receivers do have varying levels of sensitivity, this is not a major determinant of range as long as a good quality receiver is chosen from a reputable manufacturer.

One noteworthy feature of some receivers is diversity. Diversity enables a VRx to receive two (or, in theory more) video signals through

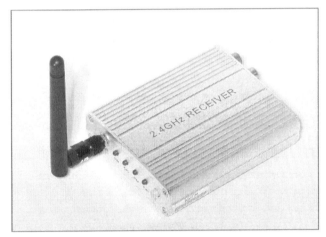

Figure 17: A standard 2.4GHz VRx

separate antennas and display the best of the two signals at any point in time. This can be done through dedicated diversity devices or is an in-built feature of some receivers. This can enable the pilot to use different antennas simultaneously to make best use of different characteristics.

5.5. Antennas

Choice of antennas for the VTx and VRx is a science in itself and has a very material impact on the quality, range and reliability of the video link. In this guide this topic will be covered in a very practical manner, enabling the reader to make sensible antenna choices without having to become an expert in the field.

Firstly, any antenna can work equally as a VTx or a VRx antenna, there aren't any antennas that only work as one or the other although different antennas are better suited as Rx or Tx antennas.

5.5.1. Key characteristics of an antenna

At a high level any antenna can be described through a small set of parameters:

a. Frequency: An antenna will usually only be appropriate for one frequency (e.g. 2.4GHz or 5.8GHz). Some pilots even have their antennas tuned to a specific channel within the frequency

b. Radiation pattern and gain: Each antenna has a specific radiation pattern. Some antennas will broadcast (or receive) equally in all directions (in which case the radiation pattern is a sphere centred around the antenna) while other, highly directional, antennas will only transmit (or receive) in a narrow cone in front of them. A good example of a directional antenna is the typical TV aerial which needs to be pointed in the right direction to work. The choice of radiation pattern depends on your style of flying (e.g. a long range flight in the same direction or a shorter range flight around the pilot) and your equipment (e.g. an antenna tracker will enable a directional antenna to always point to the plane).

The more directional an antenna is the higher its gain. A good analogy is comparing a household lightbulb (low directionality, short range) with a flashlight (high directionality, long range). Gain is measured in dBi, with unidirectional antennas having typically 1-3dBi and directional having usually 8-15dBi.

In addition to directionality, examining the radiation patterns will reveal other considerations the pilot will need to take into account. For example, even unidirectional antennas typically have a doughnut shaped pattern, with a low-sensitivity area right above and below them. As such it is common for the video signal to be weak when flying directly over the pilot.

The following diagram provides an illustration of the differences between omni and directional antennas as well as two representative actual radiation patterns ("vertical", as seen from the side and "horizontal", as seen from above)

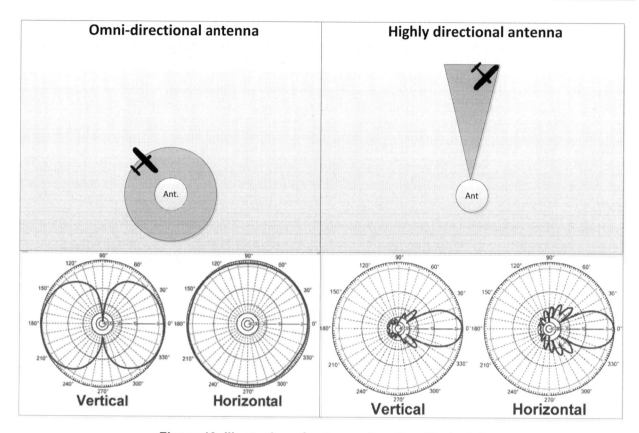

Figure 18: Illustration of antenna directionality (gain)

c. Polarisation: Antennas are either linear or circular polarised.

Linear polarised antennas are either horizontal or vertical polarised. Also, physically tilting a horizontal polarised antenna 90 degrees will make it into a vertical polarised one. For a good link it is critical that two linear polarised antennas (Tx and Rx) have the same polarisation.

The practical implication of this is that if the receiver antenna is vertically polarised (usually pointing upwards) so should the on-board transmitter antenna. The issue however occurs when the plane banks and what was previously a horizontally polarised antenna becomes a 45 degrees polarised antenna.

Circular polarised antennas (CP antennas) revolutionised FPV by removing this issue as they are neither horizontal nor vertical polarised and as such will work at any angle. The only consideration is that both antennas are either right hand circular polarised or left hand circular polarised. Note that while circular polarised antennas avoid polarisation misalignment and are significantly better at multipath rejection (see below), they usually have slightly less theoretical maximum range than a set of linear polarised antennas working in perfect conditions.

d. Multipath rejection: Multipath is an issue that occurs when the video signal reaches the receiver from multiple paths or directions. This would typically happen when the signal bounces off obstacles. Multipath can only be avoided by appropriate choice of flying location but can be significantly mitigated by use of circular polarised antennas.

e. Mounting: Finally, different types of antenna perform better when mounted in a particular way. For example a cloverleaf is best mounted on a tripod and as high from the ground as possible while a patch must be close to the ground.

5.5.2. Examples and typical combinations

The most common antenna is the "rubber duck". These are included with most receivers and transmitters and are unidirectional linear polarised antennas with a doughnut shaped radiation pattern.

Most pilots immediately swap their rubber duck antennas for unidirectional circular polarised ones such as the skew planar and cloverleaf. These are similarly unidirectional but are circular polarised and as such do not suffer from polarisation misalignment or from multipath interference. The choice of the specific unidirectional CP antenna depends on the desired radiation pattern. A typical combination is a cloverleaf for the VTx and a skew planar for the VRx.

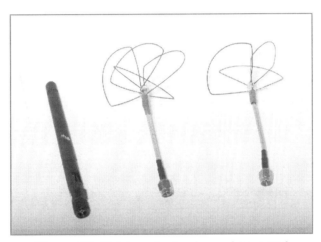

Figure 19: Rubber duck, skew planar and cloverleaf 2.4GHz antennas

The next step change in range comes with the use of directional antennas such as patch antennas. Patch antennas are small, light and offer high sensitivity (~7dBi) with a large enough radiation angle. Patch antennas can, in theory, be used without an antenna tracker as long as the pilot ensures that the plane is always flying in the right area in front of the pilot.

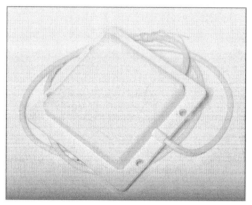

Figure 20: An 8dBi 2.4GHz right hand circularly polarised (RHCP) patch antenna

Finally there are a number of highly directional antennas, both linear polarised and CP. Examples include the yagi (typical TV antenna), helical and crosshair. These typically require an experienced pilot and/or an antenna tracker to ensure they always point towards the plane.

As new antenna designs are invented every year the reader is advised to research the latest and most appropriate choices through the online forums and online shops.

5.6. Antenna tracking

Antenna trackers are devices that enable the VRx antenna to always point towards the plane, keeping it within the antenna's most sensitive region. They come in a number of forms and using a number of technologies. This section will describe the most common setup.

Antenna trackers include a number of components:

a. On board coordinates encoder: The plane will need to transmit its GPS coordinates to the base station to inform the tracker where the plane is at any point in time. This is either a separate device or part of an OSD. In both cases the coordinates are then embedded either within the video signal or within an audio channel
b. Ground station coordinates decoder: As the coordinates are received by the VRx they need to be decoded and processed by the ground station decoder. This will typically

receive the signal through standard RCA cable from the receiver, read the coordinates, and then output the same signal for further use

c. Ground station tracker: The tracker itself is comprised of the antenna and a pan/tilt mechanism driven by two servos. The decoder controls the servos to point the antenna towards the plane. When choosing a tracker take into account the weight of your antenna (not all trackers can handle a 3kg yagi!) and choose servos that provide appropriate freedom of motion (e.g. 180 or 360 degrees)

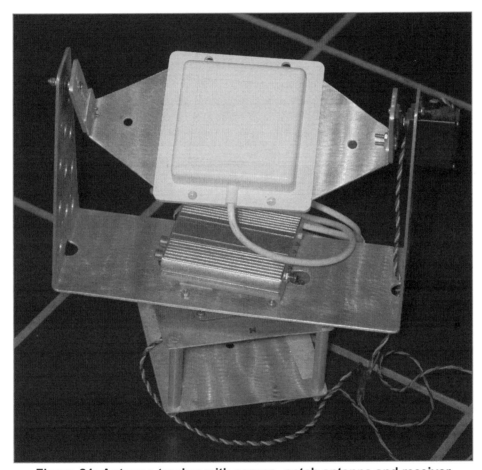

Figure 21: Antenna tracker with servos, patch antenna and receiver

Note that some antenna tracking systems don't use GPS coordinates to locate the plane. Instead they use relative strengths of the video signal to move the antenna to the position of best reception.

5.7. OSD

The on-screen display module is located on-board the plane and overlays information over the video signal produced by the camera. This can be as simple as the voltage of the battery or turn your video into an F-16 cockpit. Typical information displayed by an OSD includes:

a. Speed and altitude
b. Coordinates
c. Number of GPS satellites
d. RSSI (see section 4.6)
e. Compass
f. Battery voltage level
g. Battery milliamps used
h. Current draw
i. Which way is home
j. Distance to home

The OSD typically has a number of sensors to collect the necessary data including a current sensor (which is connected right after the battery and before any devices that consume power), GPS and pitot tube (for airspeed).

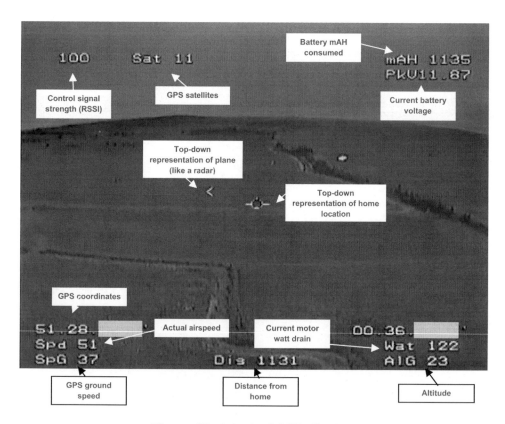

Figure 22: A typical OSD display

6. Ground station

The ground station is the element of the FPV setup that stays on the ground. Some components of it such as the control and video transmitters have already been covered. As such this section will cover the rest.

6.1. The shell

Ground station equipment could, in theory, be bundled into a spaghetti of cables and components and thrown in a plastic bag for transport and deployment. However, that is likely to end in tears as cables get pulled and components break. As such pilots typically construct their own ground station "shells" to house and transport their ground station equipment.

These can be sophisticated suitcases with built in displays, switches, cooling and all cables hidden from site. They could also be much simpler, such as an old plastic toolbox with the cables and components neatly secured within.

Figure 23: A rough DIY base station box

Figure 24: A more sophisticated ground station

6.2. Video display

An important component in any ground station is the video display. Two formats are used, goggles and screens. Both are capable of the necessary display resolution but have different characteristics

Goggles provide a more immersive experience as they block out all vision apart from the video image (which, given the proximity to the eyes can be the equivalent to a 40 inch LCD screen). They can be disorienting for some users and not all models can cater for all types of eyesight. They also make it harder to switch between FPV and 3rd person view, something which is useful for beginners.

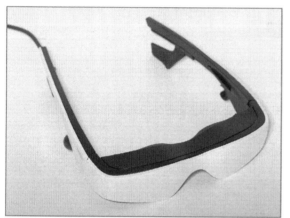
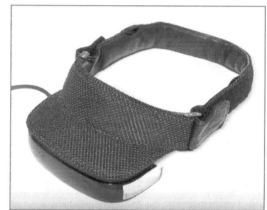

Figure 25: Two types of goggles

Monitors are standard LCD monitors with analogue video in and 12V DC power. They provide a less immersive experience and a smaller viewing area but are cheaper than goggles and enable faster switching to 3rd person view. If using a monitor it is often necessary to build a viewing box to block out sunlight.

Some setups have multiple displays to enable "passengers" to also experience the flight.

A critical characteristic of any FPV display is the avoidance of "blue screen". Many devices when faced with a low quality (but still very usable for piloting) signal will display a blue screen instead of the actual signal. This can be disastrous and should be avoided when choosing a display.

Figure 26: A 9 inch passenger LCD display

6.3. Recording

Recording the video that is being transmitted from the plane is both fun and a highly advisable safety feature for two reasons:

a. It enables the pilot to examine the video later to diagnose problems and improve their setup
b. For setups that include an OSD that displays the plane's coordinates it enables the pilot to instantly playback the last few frames before a crash, read the coordinates and then locate the plane

Many types of recording devices are available and are mostly equivalent. Key characteristics include:

a. The ability to record analogue video and be powered by DC power
b. Good recorders do not display a blue screen (see section 6.2 for more detail on blue screen)
c. The ability to play back the video on the field (without, for example, connecting to a computer)

Common types of recording devices include:

a. Digital video recorders whose sole purpose is the recording of video
b. Camcorders with analogue video in (usually older models)
c. Laptops with a video capture card or USB device. This is the least preferred option due to the time it takes to boot up, short battery life, screen glare and the potential for unpredictable behaviour

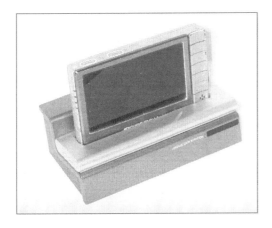

Figure 27: An "old school" Archos recorder

Figure 28: A modern DVR recorder

6.4. Video splitter

Most VRx only provide a single video out signal. A pilot will usually want to use this for multiple purposes (e.g. piloting, recording and for a "passenger"). Video splitter devices are used for enabling this. These can either be dedicated devices or part of ground station packages that some vendors provide (e.g. alongside telemetry, diversity or antenna tracking capability).

6.5. Power

A reliable and sufficient power source is critical for any ground station and although many devices (e.g. goggles or recorders) tend to have their own battery, an additional battery for the rest of the components is necessary.

A common solution is a 3 cell LiPo battery. The exact capacity required depends on equipment but 4000mAH is sufficient for most setups.

It is also likely that the ground station will need multiple power levels (12V and 5V typically) for powering various devices. An effective way of stepping down the voltage is using a standard BEC.

7. Interference

Interference is possibly the most debated topic in the hobby and minimising it a key target of any FPV pilot. Tips for minimising it have already been covered in previous sections and this section intends to provide a summary of key causes and solutions.

7.1. Identifying interference

Identifying the type and cause of interference is the first step in the process and often a bit of an art. While the most reliable way is to post a video of the interference at one of the FPV forums, this table provides some basic advice on identifying types of interference.

Symptom	Cause
Horizontal lines of significant interference sliding down the screen	This is likely a digital device broadcasting in your frequency. This is common in the 2.4GHz band which computer wireless networks use
Sudden and almost complete loss of signal for a short period	a) Possibly not interference. This is the symptom when the plane flies in the VTx/VRx blind spots (often directly above the pilot) b) Commonly, multipath interference, where the signal bounces off obstacles and reaches the receiver from multiple directions, with signals cancelling each other out c) Commonly, loss of polarisation (for linear polarised antennas), e.g. when the plane banks d) Possible interference from on-board components
Slightly blurry horizontal lines sliding down the screen	Possibly interference caused by "dirty power" caused by servos or ESCs powered by the same battery
Gradually increasing noise to signal ratio on the video image	Possibly not interference. This is the symptom of gradually flying outside of your link range or bringing obstacles within the Frensel zone between the Tx and Rx

7.2.   Resolving interference

Eliminating interference is a quest that never ends for the FPV pilot. Building an interference resistant setup should be at the heart of your FPV setup design and patiently identifying and resolving individual causes will incrementally result in a robust and reliable link.

The following table sets out some of the common causes, ways to diagnose and solutions.

Cause	Diagnostic	Solutions
Ambient noise in the video or control frequencies in the vicinity of the flying area	Change flying site and re-test or use a radio frequency meter	Change flying area Change frequency
Dirty power from servos or ESCs connected to the same battery	Only connect the video gear and check for interference	Use a filtered BEC for servos Use an LC filter Use torroids (ferrite rings) Use shielded cables for the video signal
Unexpected, sudden and temporary loss of signal	Check video when on the ground to rule out range, ambient noise or blind spot related causes Disconnect individual components to isolate the problematic component	In the case of an on-board component causing the interference the best solution is to replace it with a "quiet" one. Shielding of components, use of twisted cables and ferrite rings can also mitigate these issues
Multipath	Change flying site and retest or ensure no obstacles around and between the plane and ground station	Change flying site or style Use of circular polarised antennas

8. Flying tips

As mentioned at the outset this is not a guide to RC flying. However, FPV piloting does require some special considerations in terms of flying techniques such as:

a. Always fly with a "spotter". They will keep curious people at bay and give much needed comfort for those early FPV flights

b. Take baby steps. Always increase the complexity and range of your flying in small increments. This is especially true when making changes to an established setup. Don't try a long range flight with a new stabilisation system!

c. It is desirable to have a fallback in the event that your control signal is lost. An easy way of achieving this is to start by holding your control in a way that reduces the signal link (in most cases this means ensuring that the polarisation of your RC transmitter and receiver do not match by holding the transmitter either horizontal or vertical)

d. Altitude is important. The further away the plane is the easier it is for trees and other objects to enter the Frensel zone between Tx and Rx. If you find you're losing your link, increasing altitude is likely to help

e. Know your range limits. The range of an FPV setup is determined by different factors depending on the setup (video link, control link or batteries duration). Learn the limits of your setup by gradually testing them and fly within them. Having visibility of your RSSI (control signal strength) on your OSD will help understand control range while a battery meter will help understand battery limitations

9. Finding the plane

Crashing your plane is as upsetting as it is (almost) inevitable. An FPV setup is riddled with single points of failure and sooner or later a pilot mistake, design flaw, component malfunction or unfortunate circumstance is likely to cause a crash. The important thing is to have a robust recovery plan (and ideally a backup for that as well). This can include:

a. Recording your video link where the OSD can display coordinates: As long as the video link was lost close to the ground this is an easy way to track your plane. Using an iPhone or equivalent device with a GPS and maps. The issue of course is if signal was lost while the plane was still high up in the air

b. Using a GPS/GSM/GPRS device: These are small devices, typically used to track cars, that include a GPS and accept a mobile phone SIM card. On request the device can then send exact GPS coordinates to your mobile phone. While very straightforward the issue with this device is that it needs both a valid GPS signal and a good mobile signal to work – which may not always be the case

c. Using a UHF beacon. These devices emit a specific tone on the UHF band which can be picked up by a common walkie talkie. As they use the UHF band the signal is good for a few kilometres. The pilot can then use the walkie talkie to gradually seek out the signal, walking towards the direction where the signal becomes stronger. The difficulty is that this isn't an exact process and can take a while to locate the plane

10. Author's setup (in detail)

In this section I set out the steps I took in developing my FPV setup and the lessons learnt in the process. It is not suggested that this is the optimum path to follow but it should help highlight some of the decisions and lessons learnt in the process.

10.1. The first setup

Plane	Twinstar 2 (foam)
Control	72MHz radio
Flight cam	KX-131
Camera pan/tilt	None
Video	500mw 2.4GHz Tx
Video antennas	Rubber ducks, then CP cloverleaf and skew planar
Antenna tracker	None
Video splitter	Boss BVAM5
Batteries	Two 3S Lipos, one for control and motor and one for video link
OSD	Eagletree OSD with GPS
Stabilisation	None
Viewing device	Headplay goggles
Recording device	Laptop computer (and then an Archos 504)
Tracking device	None
HD recording	None
Other	None

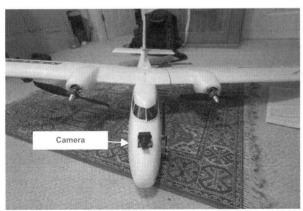

Figure 29: Author's Twinstar 2

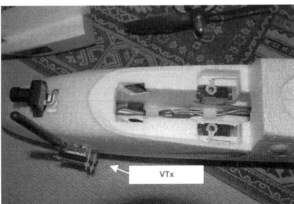

Figure 30: Clean wiring

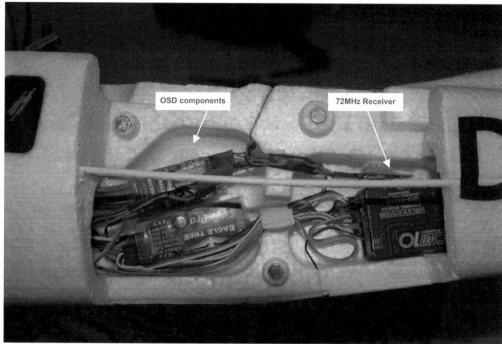

Figure 31: The FPV gear panel

Experiences and lessons learnt

This was my first FPV setup and as such I tried to keep it simple and low cost. I used my really old 72MHz radio and a simple video link. I got a decent flight cam but didn't add the complexity of pan/tilt. I did feel that an OSD was necessary to help me find my way home and I did want to experience FPV through goggles. Recording was managed through a standard laptop with a video encoding USB dongle and a low cost video splitter to feed the receiver video signal to both the goggles and laptop.

The first few flights were disasters due to mechanical, construction and basic pilot issues – nothing to do with FPV. This taught me the lesson to first test a plane fully in third person and then start with FPV.

Another issue (which resulted in a nice nose dive) was interference. My camera required 5v power so I bought a voltage regulator called Anyvolt. It took me a while and a crash to figure out that the anyvolt caused the control receiver to freeze for a couple of seconds every few seconds – which is all it takes for a total disaster.

Thankfully I had the OSD and ground station recording so could always find my plane.

Another lesson was that laptops are not ideal for recording video – they take a long time to load, the screen glares and software issues is the last thing you need on the field. So my next FPV purchase was a second hand Archos recording device which solved that problem.

One last upgrade was replacing my standard linear polarised rubber duck antennas with circular polarised cloverleaf and skew planar antennas. I highly recommend this upgrade from the outset. With this setup I dared to go within 1km or so (still within visual range).

49

10.2. Second stage

Plane	Twinstar 2 (foam)
Control	72MHz radio
Flight cam	KX-131
Camera pan/tilt	None
Video	500mw 2.4GHz Tx
Antennas	8dBi CP Patch (receiver) and cloverleaf (transmitter)
Antenna tracker	Eagletree Eagleeyes antenna tracker
Video splitter	Included with eagleeyes
Batteries	Two 3S Lipos, one for control and motor and one for video link
OSD	Eagletree OSD with GPS
Stabilisation	Copilot 2
Viewing device	Headplay goggles
Recording device	Archos 504
Tracking device	FMKit's beacon
HD recording	None
Other	None

Experiences and lessons learnt

My first setup quickly run out of video range so my next step was to invest in longer range video equipment. I installed an eagleeyes ground station (which includes both antenna tracking and video splitting), got a second hand aluminium tracker and an 8dBi CP patch antenna. This gave me many kilometres of range – well beyond my control range.

This made me nervous as my 72MHz control was expected to reach 1-2km at best. So I installed a Copilot stabilisation system and configured my OSD's return to home functionality. After a lot of testing I had a plane that would return to me if I flew out of control range or if something went wrong.

With this setup I confidently went out to over 1km and beyond line of site.

Having had a few close calls I also got a basic UHF beacon to enable me to track the plane wherever it crashed using a standard walkie talkie.

The beacon paid off a bit faster than I'd have liked. One foggy day I discovered that the Copilot stabilisation system doesn't work in fog (because it uses the infrared radiation of the horizon to calculate angle and fog blocks this). This led to the plane nose diving into a forest and stuck at the very top of a very tall tree. Thankfully after a few hours of searching with the walkie talkie I found the plane and the equipment within.

That was the end of the Twinstar.

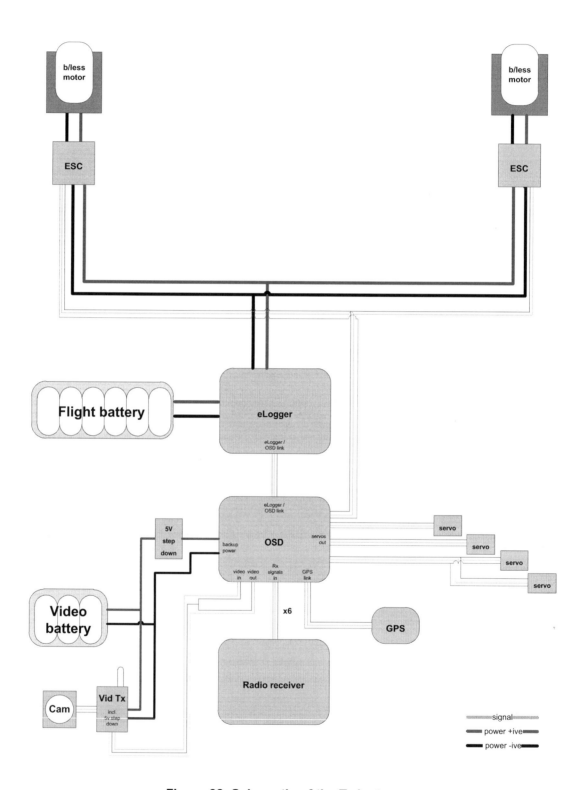

Figure 32: Schematic of the Twinstar

10.3. Third stage

Plane	Hobbyking 168 Eagle (fibreglass)
Control	Dragonlink UHF
Flight cam	690 TV lines camera
Camera pan/tilt	Pan and tilt for both flight cam and Go Pro
Video	500mw 2.4GHz Tx
Antennas	8dBi CP Patch (receiver) and cloverleaf (transmitter)
Antenna tracker	Eagletree Eagleeyes antenna tracker
Video splitter	Included with eagleeyes
Batteries	Three 3S Lipos, two for motors and one for video link and control
OSD	Eagletree OSD with GPS
Stabilisation	Guardian stabilisation
Viewing device	Headplay goggles
Recording device	Archos 504
Tracking device	FMKit's beacon
HD recording	GoPro Hero
Other	Pitot tube for airspeed indication

Experiences and lessons learnt

Having lost the Twinstar and learnt a lot from the process I designed the Eagle with care as a long range FPV plane. The main constraint previously was the control link. So I got a Dragonlink UHF to attach to a new Futaba 10 channel. I also learnt from the Copilot experience and got the Guardian, an inertial stabiliser which doesn't rely on infrared radiation.

I also redesigned the power system, splitting the motor power completely from the control and video link. This meant that even if the motor batteries run out I still had visual and control.

Once the plane was built, tested and tuned I had myself a rock solid FPV platform. After this point my attention was on optimising performance through mechanics (e.g. adding flaps for softer landings, adjusting the CG), range, durability, tuning the stabilisation and return to home and of course enjoying the experience knowing that I can rely on my equipment.

I've since had loads of successful flights across the country and the plane still flies strong. I've been as far out as 5km with a stable video and control signal, flown fast and close to the ground and above water. It took two years to reach this point but absolutely worth it.

Figure 33: The Eagle in flight

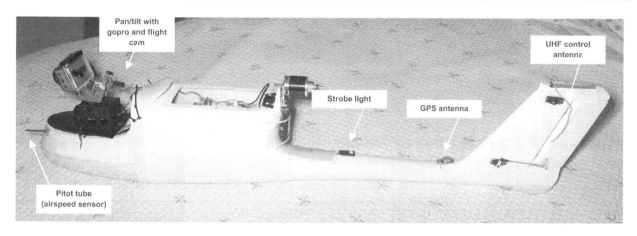

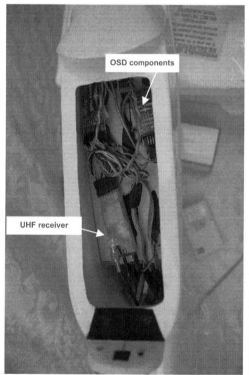

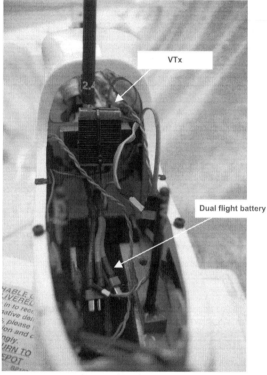

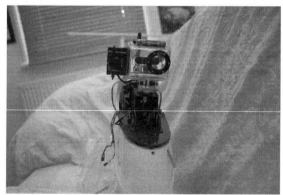

Figure 34: Collection of Eagle photos

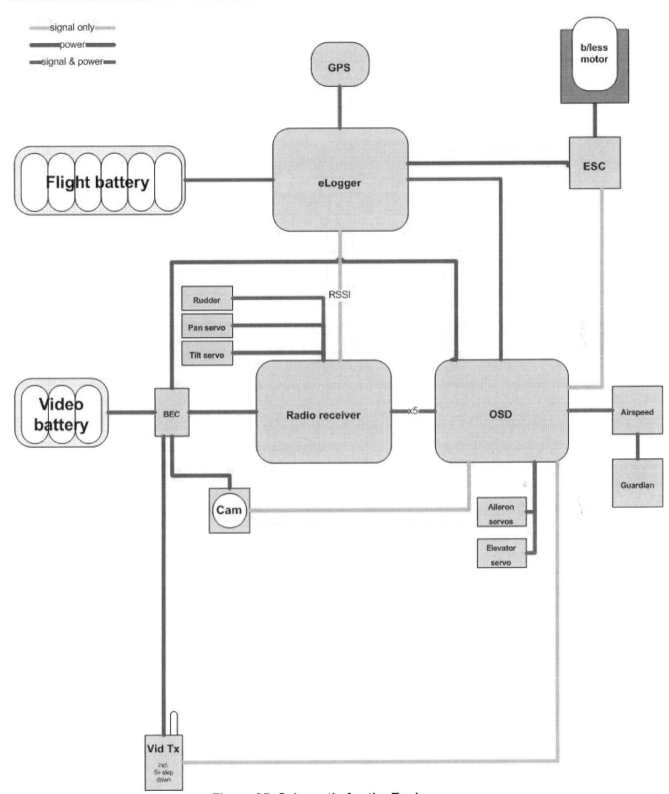

signal only
power
signal & power

Figure 35: Schematic for the Eagle

10.4. Fourth stage

Plane	Zephyr II
Control	Dragonlink UHF
Flight cam	690 TV lines camera
Camera pan/tilt	None
Video	500mw 2.4GHz Tx
Antennas	10dBi crosshair and cloverleaf (transmitter)
Antenna tracker	Eagletree Eagleeyes antenna tracker
Video splitter	Included with Eagleeyes
Batteries	Two 4S LiPos for motors and one 3S for video link and control
OSD	Eagletree OSD with GPS
Stabilisation	Guardian stabilisation
Viewing device	Cinemizer OLEDs with ski mask mod
Recording device	Mini DVR
Tracking device	FMKit's beacon
HD recording	GoPro Hero
Other	Pitot tube for airspeed indication

Experiences and lessons learnt

The Eagle was good fun and served me well for a number of months. But it left me wishing for three things. Firstly, the Eagle took over 15 minutes to setup (and that's the plane only), which I wanted to avoid. Secondly, I wanted something a lot more nimble, something I could fly close to the ground, between objects and have some fun with. Thirdly, I needed something that could take a lot more rough landings than the Eagle could handle. It was clear I what I needed was a wing, and the Zephyr 2 is a classic choice. It did mean losing the pan and tilt but that's a sacrifice I was willing to make.

Figure 37: The Zephyr II

Other changes to the setup included replacing my 8dBi patch with a 10dBi crosshair. This not only gave me an extra 2dBi but has a nice and wide radiation pattern too.

The Archos, whilst effective, was far too cumbersome so I replaced it with a compact mini DVR. The headplays were relegated for use by any "passengers" I may have from time to time and my primary goggles became the Cinemizer OLEDs which give a far superior image. Their only issue was that they are designed for indoor use and hence allowed a lot of light through around the sides of the glasses. To resolve this I installed them inside of a ski mask to completely block all light.

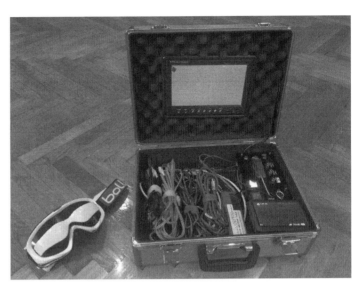

Figure 38: The new base station

Finally, in the spirit of portability, I installed all my new gear in a compact aluminium case.

The net result was just as good as expected. The whole setup could be deployed in a matter of minutes and the Zephyr took my FPV experience to a new, adrenaline packed, level. Many crashes later it still flies strong.

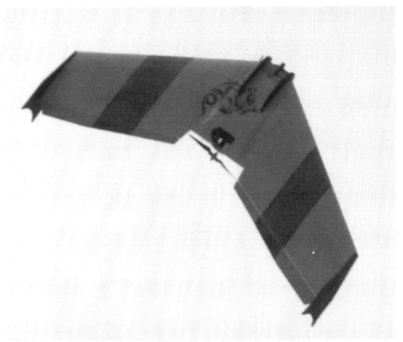

Figure 39: The ZII flying overhead

11. Advanced and ancillary topics

11.1. Link margin

Link margin is a telecommunications term used to describe whether a given wireless system has enough power/sensitivity to communicate a signal under given circumstances.

Specifically, link margin, expressed in dB, is the additional headroom that the system has. A system with link margin of ≥ 0 is expected, under the given theoretical conditions, to work. A system with <0 is not expected to work.

For example, a wireless system with a link margin of 10dB is expected to be able to handle up to an additional 10dB of attenuation.

Link margin calculation is straightforward and the formula is as follows:

Link margin =
    Min(- Rx_sensitivity , Noise_floor) + Rx_antenna_gain + Tx_transmitted_power + Tx_antenna_gain – free_space_loss

So, as expected, the higher the sensitivity, gain or power, the higher the margin and the farther away the Tx is from the Rx, the lower the margin.

With this formula a pilot can calculate the theoretical maximum range of their system. Note that reality often diverges marginally from the theoretical calculations and as such it is advisable to always allow a few additional dB of margin.

Lets take, as an example, the author's latest Zephyr 2 setup:

Rx sensitivity

Rx sensitivity is measured in dB and may be stated in the specification of your receiver. Where this is not known -85dB is a good assumption. Note that Rx sensitivity is expressed in negative dB and as such the link margin formula includes "-(Rx sensitivity)".

We'll use -85dB for our calculation.

Noise floor

Noise floor is the level of ambient noise at our chosen frequency, affecting our system, and specifically our Rx. The only way to know the noise floor at a given location is to measure it at the location. As this is not practical for most pilots an assumption must be made.

If the noise floor (in dB) is higher than your receiver's sensitivity then the noise floor would drown any signals that would be picked up by the receiver's sensitivity beyond the noise floor.

For example, a receiver with 95dB sensitivity operating in an area with a noise floor of 85dB would be effectively operating at 85dB.

In our example, we will assume that we fly in a remote area with a noise floor that does not affect our system, say 95dB.

Rx antenna gain

Rx antenna gain is measured in dB and is always stated on your antenna's radiation plot. In our example we're using a crosshair antenna with a gain of 10dB.

Tx transmitted power

Transmitted power is a function of the transmitter's watt rating. The watt rating is converted into dB using the below graph[15].

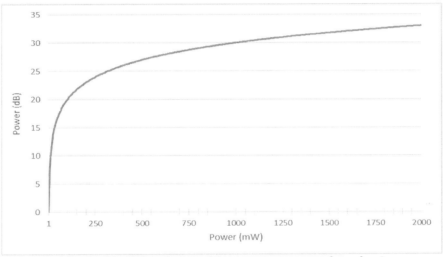

Figure 40: Video transmitter power conversion chart

A table of the most common transmitter powers is also provided below.

mw	db
25	13.9794
200	23.0103
500	26.9897
1000	30
1500	31.76091

In our example we're using a 500mW transmitter and as such the Tx transmitted power is 26.97dB

---

[15] The actual formula is dB = 10 * (log10 (mW)) where log 10 is log with base 10.

Tx antenna gain

Tx antenna gain is measured in dB and is always stated on your antenna's radiation plot. In our example we're using a cloverleaf antenna with a gain of 1.26dB.

Free space loss

This is the signal loss due to the signal traveling through the air. It assumes no obstacles and is affected by the actual distance between the plane and the receiver as well as the system's frequency. As you can see in the following table, the higher the frequency, the higher the loss[16].

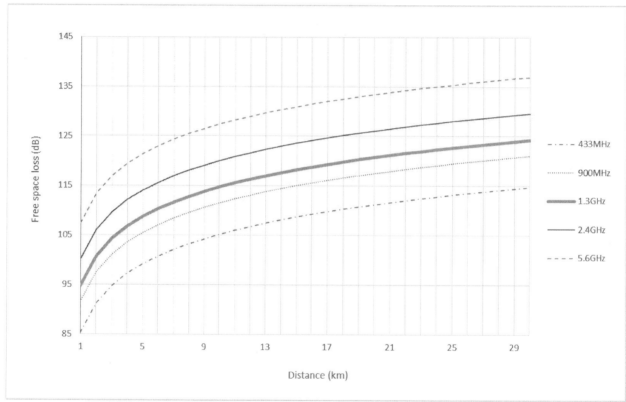

Figure 41: Loss due to distance chart

In our example we're flying at 2.4GHz and lets assume we're flying at 10km. This gives us a loss of -119.

Putting it all together

So, for our system, the link margin is equal to:

= Min(-(-85),(95)) + 10 + 26.97 + 1.26 – 119
= 85 + 10 + 26.97 + 1.26 -119
= 4.23dB

---

[16] The actual formula is FreeSpaceLoss = 20log10(d) + 20log10(f) + 32.45 where d is distance in km and f is frequency in MHz

So, our system has a link margin of 4.23dB. Looking at our loss due to distance chart we can see that this can get us, in theory, up to an additional 5km in range.

Reversing the formula

A useful way to look at the link margin formula is to see what your maximum theoretical range is. To do this we can rearrange the formula as follows:

Free_space_loss =
    Min(-Rx_sensitivity,Noise_floor) + Rx_antenna_gain + Tx_transmitted_power +
Tx_antenna_gain – link_margin

We then set link margin to zero (as we're looking for the maximum range at which the margin drops to zero) gives us:

Free_space_loss =
Min(-Rx_sensitivity,Noise_floor) + Rx_antenna_gain + Tx_transmitted_power +
Tx_antenna_gain

Once we calculate the loss due to distance we then use the chart above to convert it into actual distance.

In our example:
Free_space_loss =
85 + 10 + 26.97 + 1.26 = 123.23dB

Which, using the graph, gives us a maximum theoretical range of just under 16km. When using these kinds of calculations however, it is advisable to always allow a few additional dB to cater for other factors.

Useful observations

Three useful observations can be drawn from the link margin calculations:
   a) Noise floor can have a dramatic effect on your system as it effectively caps the sensitivity of your receiver. This is especially important when using directional antennas where the noise floor may change as the antenna changes direction. If, for example, the plane flies over a populated area, then the noise floor may increase to the point where link margin turns negatice.
   b) Power gives diminishing returns. As you can see from the relevant graph, the relationship of power (watts) and transmitted power (dB) is logarithmic, i.e. increasing the power gives less and less increase in transmitted power. That is why most pilots use 500-700mW of power. Using higher power (e.g. 1W) would give a small increase in transmitted power (e.g. 3dB) but may be introducing overwhelming interference to the rest of the plane's systems.
   c) Pick the right frequency. Earlier on in the guide it was established that lower frequencies give higher range. This is now evident when looking at the loss due to distance graph. In our example, if we'd swapped our 2.4GHz system for 5.8GHz, this would result in a reduction in range of approximately 12km!

11.2. Ground loops

Simply put, a ground loop is the situation where different ground (in our case, negative) wires have different potentials. This happens when a component has multiple ways to reach the battery's ground and when these different ways have a different resistance (e.g. because of the wires used or because of other components interjected along the path).

The result of ground loops can vary. Many of them can be harmless, others can cause interference to the video signal while in extreme cases a loop could cause components to malfunction.

A frequent ground loop in FPV setups and one that can cause trouble is when the receiver is grounded both through the built-in BEC of an ESC and through another route (e.g. its connection to an autopilot or stabilisation system). The ground from the ESC's BEC is likely to be noisier and can spread interference to the video signal. To avoid this it is highly advisable to use a separate, d

This is demonstrated in the simplified diagram below.

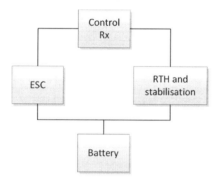

Figure 42: Simplified ground loop example

11.3. Special considerations for multicopters

Whilst all advice and guidance provided in this guide applies equally to all types of FPV crafts, multicopters in particular do require additional attention as they are subject to some constraints unique to this type of craft.

a) There is often very limited space which often results in components which would normally be far away from each other to be placed in close proximity of each other. For example, the control Rx, VTx, ESCs and GPS antenna are all likely to be within a few centimetres of each other. As such additional care should be taken to minimise interference by careful positioning, choice of quality components, appropriate cabling and, if required, shielding. It is not uncommon for the GPS receiver to be placed on a rigid pole above the rest of the multicopter to avoid this issue.

b) The VTx antenna will often be obstructed by other parts of the multicopter, even if positioned as far away as possible. This will become apparent when flying when video signal will rapidly deteriorate when the craft is at a specific angle to the VRx and facing in a specific direction. A simple rotation of the craft will then rapidly improve the signal. When positioning the antenna take care to avoid the battery and excessive amounts of carbon fibre blocking the signal path

c) Unlike planes which can glide and self correct to a good degree, multicopters are kept afloat by the constant operation of the controller, GPS, ESCs and motors. For many pilots good GPS reception is critical (although multis can operate without a GPS in the first place) and as such correct positioning of the GPS is important.

d) Due to their complexity and inherently unstable nature, multicopters can be prone to accidents and those accidents tend to expensive. All it takes for a multi to crash is a single failed connection, failed ESC, cracked prop or incorrect controller configuration. Multis are less forgiving than planes, cars or boats and as such should be built with additional care and attention to detail and should be tested thoroughly before any serious FPV flights are attempted.

11.4. Alternative video links

The standard video link used by vast majority of pilots is standard definition analogue video. However two alternatives are also emerging.

3D video
With relatively small adjustments the standard kit can be transformed to deliver a 3D experience to the pilot. This can be a lot more immersive, especially when piloting multicopters and ground vehicles.

3D video transmission is obtained by having two standard flight cams instead of one, separated by a few centimetres, each transmitting the image that each of the eyes should see. An additional processing stage is required to combine the two video feeds into a single one. This can result in the two images being placed side by side (which results in a loss of horizontal resolution) or to alternate frames between the two sources (which results in a loss of actual frame rate).

This is then transmitted as normal via the VTx and received by the VRx. Regarding display, 3D necessitates the use of goggles and most models support various 3D modes.

High definition (HD) video
The dream of many FPV pilots is to be able to experience the same video quality and resolution when flying as they do when viewing their recorded HD videos. In short, having live HD video from the flight cam all the way to the goggles.

To achieve this most components of the video link need to be specifically designed for HD. The camera should capture in HD, the VTx should transmit in digital HD, the VRx should receive digital HD video and the video playback device should be able to display HD.

At the time of writing, whilst experimental attempts have been made successfully, they have been limited to very short range. However, well known FPV suppliers have already made announcements of HD-capable systems so watch this space closely[17].

---

[17] Note that in the commercial/defence space, HD video links are available. However they are priced in

11.5. Video editing and sharing

One of the usual keepsakes of an FPV flight is the high definition video. This provides a much higher quality view of the flight and one that pilots often want to share with others. It is common for pilots to edit their videos before sharing (to make them shorter, focus on the highlights and perhaps add music). This can be accomplished with simple free software or professional level video editing suites.

Video editing is an art in its own right and each person has their own objectives and style, so what follows is a short list of suggestions to bear in mind when preparing your video:

a) Try to keep videos to under 4 minutes. Unless the topic is absolutely unique and exciting people tend to skip through longer videos

b) Music, especially if synchronised with the video, can really boost the feel of a recording. However, be mindful of music copyright and the policy of any sites you intend to share the video on

c) Try to remove parts of the recording where nothing interesting happens. If you're showing the approach to some landmark of interest then many short clips of the journey in succession are often better than the whole thing (even in fast forward)

d) Aim for each scene in your clip to offer something to the viewer. This may be some context (e.g. setup and launch), exciting flying (e.g. formation flying), beautiful scenery or interesting landmarks and objects

e) When exporting your edited clip make sure you use the right settings to keep the quality of the original video

f) Stability is important. When flying we tend to tolerate a lot of sudden movements but when viewing a flight video it is important for the footage to be smooth and stable

Regarding sharing, pilots commonly use www.youtube.com and, if a more flexible platform is required, www.vimeo.com.

---

the region of thousands of dollars and hence are not being considered for FPV use.

"For once you have tasted flight you will walk the earth with your eyes turned skywards, for there you have been and there you will long to return"

Leonardo da Vinci

Made in the USA
San Bernardino, CA
18 January 2015